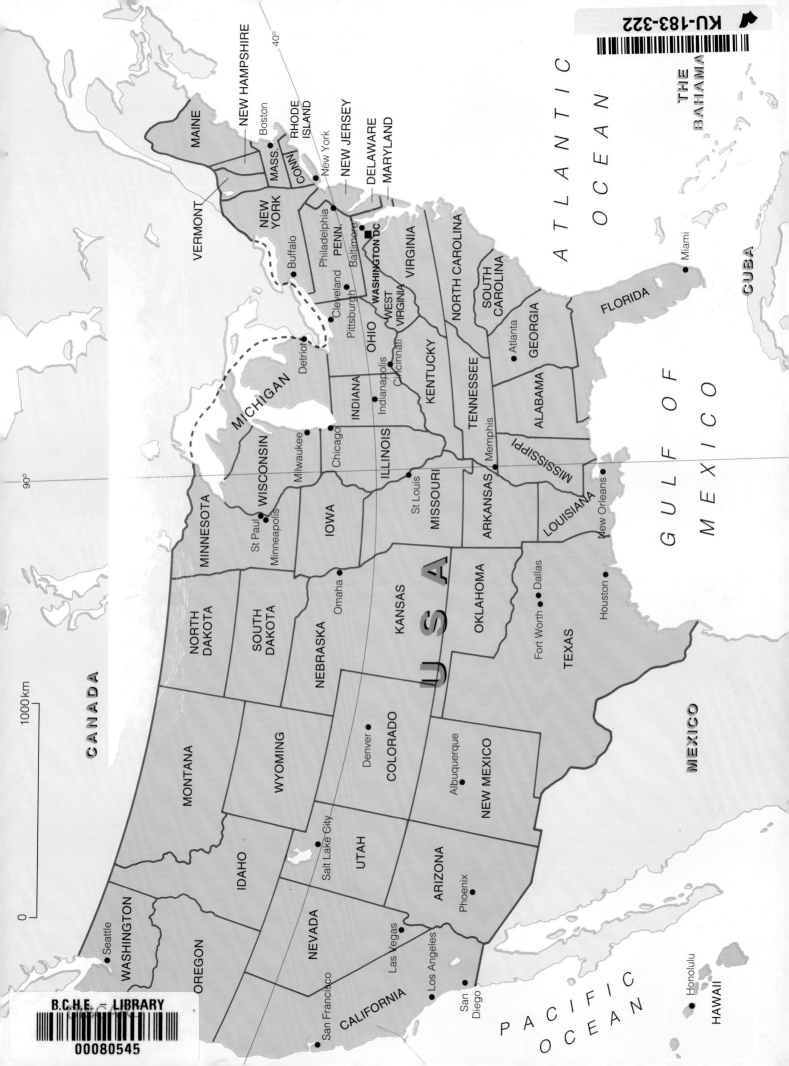

ATLANTIC

OCEAN

CUBA

CANADA

MAINE

NEW HAMPSHIRE

Boston

VERMONT

RHODE ISLAND

MASS.

CONN

NEW YORK

NEW JERSEY

New York

DELAWARE

MARYLAND

Buffalo

PENN.

Philadelphia

Baltimore

WASHINGTON DC

Cleveland

Pittsburgh

WEST VIRGINIA

VIRGINIA

OHIO

NORTH CAROLINA

Cincinnati

Detriot

INDIANA

Indianapolis

KENTUCKY

SOUTH CAROLINA

MICHIGAN

GEORGIA

Atlanta

FLORIDA

Miami

Milwaukee

Chicago

ILLINOIS

TENNESSEE

ALABAMA

WISCONSIN

Memphis

MISSISSIPPI

St Paul

Minneapolis

IOWA

St Louis

MISSOURI

ARKANSAS

LOUISIANA

New Orleans

MINNESOTA

GULF OF

MEXICO

NORTH DAKOTA

SOUTH DAKOTA

NEBRASKA

Omaha

KANSAS

U S A

OKLAHOMA

Fort Worth

Dallas

Houston

TEXAS

MONTANA

WYOMING

COLORADO

Denver

NEW MEXICO

Albuquerque

MEXICO

IDAHO

Salt Lake City

UTAH

ARIZONA

Phoenix

1000 km

0

NEVADA

Las Vegas

Los Angeles

San Diego

WASHINGTON

Seattle

OREGON

San Francisco

CALIFORNIA

Honolulu

HAWAII

PACIFIC

OCEAN

40°

90°

First published in 1992 by Simon & Schuster Young Books
Text © John Baines 1992
Illustration © Simon & Schuster Young Books 1992

Simon & Schuster Young Books
Campus 400
Maylands Avenue
Hemel Hempstead
Herts HP2 7EZ

Design	Roger Kohn
Editor	Penny Clarke
DTP editor	Helen Swansbourne
Picture research	Valerie Mulcahy
Illustration	János Márffy
	Coral Mula
Consultant	David Barrs
Commissioning editor	Debbie Fox

We are grateful to the following for permission
to reproduce photographs:
Front Cover: Telegraph Colour Library *above,* Zefa (J Tobias)
below; Susan Griggs Agency, page 22 (LeRoy Roodson);
Robert Harding Picture Library, pages 11 *below,* 15, 28 *above,*
32, 41; The Image Bank, pages 14 (Co Rentmeester),
17 (Elyse Lewin), 23 (C L Chryslin), 25 (Andy Caulfield),
28 *below* (Sobel/Klonsky), 20 (Steve Proehl), 30 (Harald
Sund), 31 (Guido A Rossi), 35 *above* (Al Satterwhite);
Roger Kohn, page 12; Magnum, pages 8 (Thomas Hoepker),
16 (Burt Clinn), 18 (Alex Webb), 36 (Michael K Nichols);
42 *below* (Alex Webb); Tony Stone Worldwide, pages 11 *above*
(Tony Craddock), 21 (Mike Powell), 24 (Dennis O'Clair), 26,
27, 35 *below* (John Darling), 37 (Chris Kapolka), 38 (John
Lawlor), 39 (David Hanson); Zefa, pages 8/9, 13, 19, 20, 33
(M M Lawrence); Zefa/Allstock, page 42 *above* (C Krebs).

Printed and bound in Hong Kong by Wing King Tong

A CIP catalogue record for this book is available from
the British Library

ISBN: 0 7500 1066 5

Words that are explained in the glossary are printed in
SMALL CAPITALS the first time they are mentioned in the text.

CONTENTS

THE
USA

John Baines

SIMON & SCHUSTER
LONDON • SYDNEY • NEW YORK • TOKYO • SINGAPORE • TORONTO

INTRODUCTION

The United States of America is the richest and most powerful country in the world. Only 5 per cent of the world's 5300 million people are Americans, but most have been influenced by them. For example, one of the USA's best known products, Coca Cola, is sold in over 170 countries.

One of the ways people learn about the USA is through the films and television programmes which are made there. They are shown around the world, usually dubbed or with sub-titles in countries where English is not the main language. People get many impressions of what America might be like from them. Depending on what they are watching it can be the countryside, the excitement of American football, the crime in the cities or the tremendous military power of the country.

How accurate are these impressions? This book will help you learn more about the USA, from its scenery to its international trade.

Why is it important to learn about the USA? The USA is the most powerful country in the world. It designs and makes the most powerful weapons and through its military power it can protect those countries that support it and threaten those that do not. It has some of the world's main industrial corporations with factories in

▲ Not all Americans are wealthy. This home in the 'boom' state of Texas is a sharp contrast to the suburban house (right). Many country people in the South are very poor.

many countries and through its economic power it influences the economies of other countries. Americans believe in DEMOCRACY and CAPITALISM. Most believe that the American way of life is the best. The influence of the USA is so strong that it can overwhelm and destroy traditional customs in other countries.

No country can afford to ignore the USA, although it is sometimes envied because of its wealth and at other times hated because of its power and influence.

THE USA AT A GLANCE

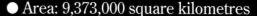

- Area: 9,373,000 square kilometres
- Population: 248.7 million (1990 census) but estimates suggest there are really 254.9 million people
- Density: 26.5 people per square kilometre
- Capital: Washington, District of Columbia, population 3 million
- Other main cities: New York 7.3 million, Los Angeles 3.4 million, Chicago 2.7 million, Philadelphia 1.5 million, Detroit 1.0 million, San Francisco 1.0 million, Dallas 1.0 million
- Highest mountain: Mt McKinley, Alaska, 6193 metres
- Language: English
- Main religion: Christianity
- Currency: US dollar, written as $ or US$
- Economy: Highly industrialised
- Major resources: Coal, oil, minerals, timber, agricultural land
- Major products: Corn, wheat, soya beans, cotton, tobacco, livestock, automobiles, electrical and electronic goods, coal, oil, gas, iron and steel, minerals, machinery
- Environmental problems: Severe pollution of air, water and land near industrial areas, soil erosion, deforestation, loss of wild areas

◀ *The USA is a wealthy country and many people can afford large detached homes and gardens in the suburbs.*

THE LANDSCAPE

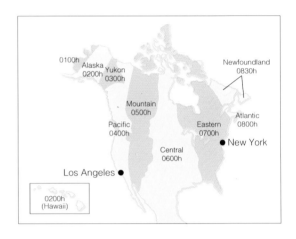

Only the former Soviet Union, Canada and China cover larger areas than the USA.

The USA is made up of 50 states, although two, Alaska and Hawaii, are separated from the other 48. Alaska lies north-west of Canada, partly within the Arctic Circle. Hawaii is a group of sub-tropical islands in the Pacific Ocean about 3,400 kilometres off the Californian coast.

In the east there is a narrow plain along the Atlantic coast. Behind the plain are the Appalachian Mountains with low rounded ridges and shallow valleys.

To the west of the Appalachians the Central Lowlands stretch across to the Rocky Mountains. The lowlands are generally flat or gently rolling and include the Great Plains. The Missouri-Mississippi rivers flow 5,971 kilometres from the lowlands into the

▲ *The USA is divided into 9 time zones. People on the west coast are 3 hours behind their friends on the east coast.*

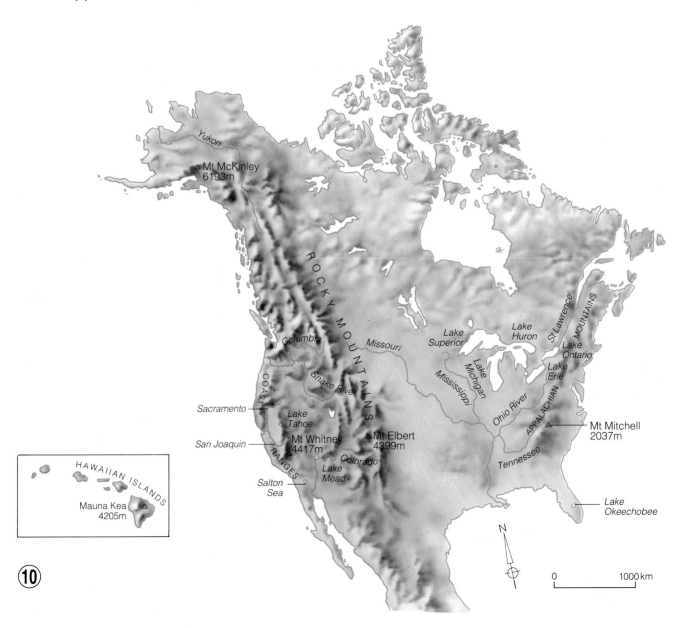

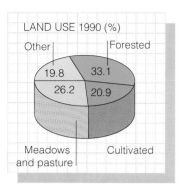

LAND USE 1990 (%)

Other 19.8
Forested 33.1
26.2
20.9
Meadows and pasture
Cultivated

▲ *The spectacular Grand Canyon in Arizona was cut by the Colorado River. It is 445 kilometres long, 1.6 kilometres deep and up to 29 kilometres wide.*

▼ *The huge swampy area of Florida called the Everglades is home to many rare species. Part is protected as a national park.*

Gulf of Mexico through the Mississippi delta. In the north-east are the Great Lakes. Lakes Superior, Huron, Erie, and Ontario are shared with Canada. The whole of the fifth, Lake Michigan, is in the USA. The Niagara Falls are between Lakes Erie and Ontario.

The Rocky Mountains rise steeply from the Great Plains and the peaks are snow covered. To the west are the plateaus and basins with spectacular land forms such as the Grand Canyon. Along the west coast are the Coast Ranges. These mountains are higher than the Appalachians. They are formed along a zone where two plates of the earth's crust collide. Movements of the plates cause regular earthquakes and volcanic activity. A huge earthquake in 1906 destroyed much of San Francisco. In 1989 a weaker one killed people and caused much damage at nearby Santa Cruz.

How warm places are depends on their distance from the equator, distance from the sea and height above sea level.

At Barrow, Alaska, which is near the Arctic Circle, the average daily temperature only rises above freezing point for three months a year. At Miami, Florida, close to the tropics, the average temperature in January is 18°C.

Temperatures decrease with altitude. In California you can sunbathe on the beach in the morning and then go skiing in the Sierra Nevada only 200 kilometres away.

The difference between the summer and winter temperatures is greater inland than on the coast. The difference at New Orleans, 50 kilometres from the Gulf of Mexico, is 16°C. At Chicago, 1,000 kilometres from the sea, the range is 28°C.

Differences in precipitation (rainfall, sleet and snow) are just as great. Warm winds blowing from the Pacific Ocean bring about 150 centimetres of rain to the states of Oregon and Washington. Once the winds reach the Great Plains they are dry and rainfall is only about 40 centimetres. The interior gets most of its rain in summer when warm moist winds are drawn in from the Gulf of Mexico.

In the south-west of the country there is hot desert. Phoenix in Arizona has less then 2 centimetres of rain a year. The cold tundra areas of the north are also very dry.

San Francisco is known for its fog which forms when warm air from the land moves out over the cool sea. The same happens off the coast of New England.

All parts of the USA suffer from the effects of extreme climate and weather conditions. Drought is one example. The Mid-west has suffered three droughts this century, the last in the late 1980s when farmers lost most of their crops. Hurricanes are another problem and occur more often than droughts. They are huge tropical storms that develop over the Gulf of Mexico and strike the south and east coasts. Inland, there are storms called tornadoes, or 'twisters', because the air spirals upwards sucking dust and debris with it.

▼ *The warm, wet sub-tropical climate of Hawaii encourages luxuriant plant growth.*

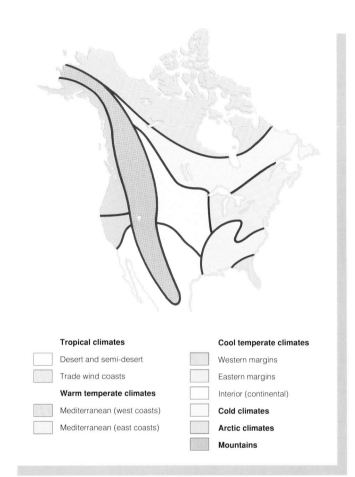

Tropical climates

☐	Desert and semi-desert
☐	Trade wind coasts

Warm temperate climates

☐	Mediterranean (west coasts)
☐	Mediterranean (east coasts)

Cool temperate climates

☐	Western margins
☐	Eastern margins
☐	Interior (continental)

Cold climates

Arctic climates

Mountains

▲ *Within the USA are some of the coldest hottest, dryest, wettest and windiest places on Earth.*

▲ *Lakes in Alaska freeze over during the long, cold winters but fishermen make holes through the ice to catch fish.*

KEY FACTS

● In the deserts the temperature can rise to 50°C during the daytime and fall to freezing point during the night.

● Wind speeds in tornadoes or 'twisters' can reach over 300 kph.

● It is so cold over most of Alaska that only the top few centimetres of the ground thaw in summer.

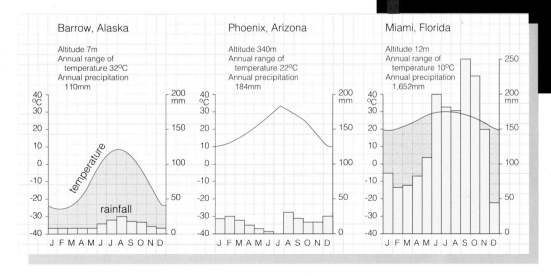

Barrow, Alaska
Altitude 7m
Annual range of temperature 32°C
Annual precipitation 110mm

Phoenix, Arizona
Altitude 340m
Annual range of temperature 22°C
Annual precipitation 184mm

Miami, Florida
Altitude 12m
Annual range of temperature 10°C
Annual precipitation 1,652mm

◄ *Florida's warm winters are popular with tourists. Barrow is too cold and Phoenix too dry.*

NATURAL RESOURCES

The USA is very rich in natural resources. It has large supplies of timber, fuels and minerals. However, consumption of resources is so high that supplies of some have to be imported.

Most of the 532 million cubic metres of timber cut down in the USA each year comes from the mountain areas of the north-west. Conservationists criticise the timber industry for clearing large areas of trees, not replanting fast enough and removing ancient forests. Alaska also has an important timber industry.

Oil and gas are found in several states including Pennsylvania, Kentucky, Oklahoma, Kansas, Texas, Louisiana, California and Alaska. After the former Soviet Union, the USA is the biggest producer of both oil and gas. So great is the demand for oil that it is mined in such inhospitable areas as around Prudhoe Bay on the north Alaskan coast. A pipeline has been built 1280 kilometres across Alaska to Valdez on the south coast to take the oil to a port that is not blocked by ice in winter.

The other major fuel is coal. Almost 889 million tonnes are mined a year and 88 million tonnes are exported. The oldest mining areas are in the Appalachians and to the south of the Great Lakes. More recently mines have been opened in the Rocky Mountains and the northern Great Plains. Although this coal is of a lower quality it is cheaper to mine and contains less sulphur.

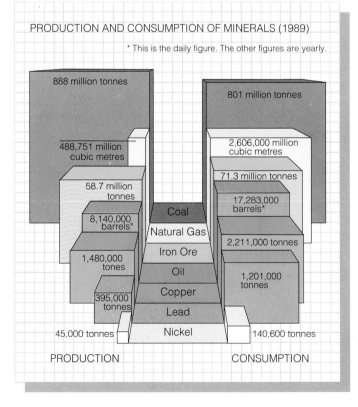

PRODUCTION AND CONSUMPTION OF MINERALS (1989)

* This is the daily figure. The other figures are yearly.

PRODUCTION		CONSUMPTION
888 million tonnes	Coal	801 million tonnes
488,751 million cubic metres	Natural Gas	2,606,000 million cubic metres
58.7 million tonnes	Iron Ore	71.3 million tonnes
8,140,000 barrels*	Oil	17,283,000 barrels*
1,480,000 tones	Copper	2,211,000 tonnes
395,000 tonnes	Lead	1,201,000 tonnes
45,000 tonnes	Nickel	140,600 tonnes

Open-cast mines like this at Gillette, Wyoming, can produce coal cheaply but they damage the environment unless the land is restored afterwards.

Sulphur is released into the atmosphere when coal is burnt. It is a major cause of acid rain.

Mineral ores are used to supply industry with metals. Iron ore is mined from the hills around the western shores of Lake Superior. Although almost 59 million tonnes are mined in the USA, the country uses over 71 million tonnes. Most of this is imported from Canada and South America.

Many other ores are mined to produce copper, aluminium, lead, zinc, silver, platinum and gold. The mines are in the mountain areas of the west.

KEY FACTS

● The tallest redwood tree is 112 metres high, more than twice the height of Nelson's Column in London.

● The world's first offshore oil wells were made in the Gulf of Mexico in 1938.

● Alaska is so cold that the oil in the pipeline between Prudhoe Bay and Valdez has to be heated so it will flow easily.

● Coal trains up to 1.5 kilometres long carry 10,000 tonnes of coal at a time.

● The Bingham Canyon Copper Mine in the Rocky Mountains has excavated a hole more than 3 kilometres across and 700 metres deep.

● Americans use twice as much energy today as 30 years ago.

▲*A giant sequoia in the Mariposa Grove near Yosemite in California. You can walk though the tree's trunk.*

THE NATIVE AMERICANS

Five hundred years ago, the area that is now the USA was occupied by little more than a million people. These native Americans were descendants of people who had migrated from Asia about 20,000 years earlier. The Inuit (or Eskimos as they used to be called) live in the cold northern areas. Those living in the mainland area are known as American Indians, once called 'Red Indians'. Originally, there were many tribes of Indians, such as the Apache, Navajo and Sioux.

European settlers who arrived from the 16th century onwards destroyed the native people and their ways of life. Today there are estimated to be 254.9 million Americans but only 1.5 million native Americans.

IMMIGRATION

The majority of Americans are descended from European emigrants. Place names often indicate from which countries the early settlers came. In the north-east there are English-sounding place names such as New Hampshire, New York and Boston. In the South there are French names such as New Orleans and Baton Rouge and in California Spanish names such as Los Angeles and San Francisco. Although English is the official language, it is not the first language for 20 per cent of the population. Cities like Miami are almost bi-lingual with English and Spanish spoken. Other languages spoken are German, Italian, French and Polish.

The next largest ethnic group are Black Americans or Afro-Americans. They form about 12 per cent of the population. They are descendants of the slaves who were brought from West Africa to work in the

▼ *The Statue of Liberty in New York symbolized for millions of immigrants a country in which they could be free.*

plantations of the South. After the abolition of slavery many moved north to find employment in large cities like Detroit, Washington DC, New York and Chicago.

During the 1970s, 1.6 million people came from Asia alone to settle in the USA.

Immigration today is more carefully controlled and only about half a million people a year are allowed to settle.

SPREAD OF SETTLEMENT

The first settlement was in the east. When a territory reached a population of 60,000 it

▲ *Wherever their ancestors came from, these children are all Americans.*

▼ *Before becoming US citizens all immigrants say: 'I pledge allegiance to the flag of the United Sates of America and the Republic for which it stands, one nation under God indivisible with liberty and justice for all.'*

KEY FACTS

● There were 4 million slaves in the USA at the time of the Civil War, 1861–65.

● 43 million people live in the north-eastern conurbation.

● Between 1900 and 1910 the USA received 8.8 million immigrants.

● Mohawk Indians erect most of the steel frames for skyscrapers in New York.

● The Sears Tower in Chicago is the highest building in the USA. It has 110 floors and is 442 metres high. It uses as much electricity as a town of 150,000 people.

● A Dutch trading company purchased Manhattan from the Native Americans in 1625 and called it Nieuw Amsterdam.

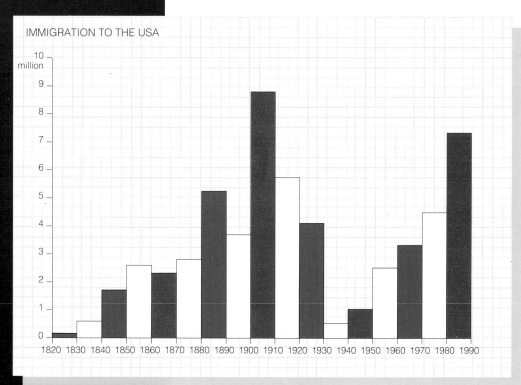

IMMIGRATION TO THE USA

could become a state. The completion of the transcontinental railway in 1869 enabled the development of the Great Plains and encouraged more people to 'Go West'.

URBAN AMERICA

Three-quarters of Americans live in cities. There are three areas where the cities have grown so large that they form huge CONURBATIONS where one city merges into the next. The first stretches between Boston and Washington DC and includes the largest city, New York. It is nicknamed Bosneywash! Although the area only covers 2 per cent of the USA, 20 per cent of Americans live in it. The second area is where many industries grew up in the 19th and early 20th centuries. It stretches between Chicago and Pittsburgh. The third stretches between San Francisco and San Diego. This is a newer area and has fewer cities, but vast areas of suburbs sprawl over the landscape.

The street pattern in most American cities is like a grid. In New York all the roads

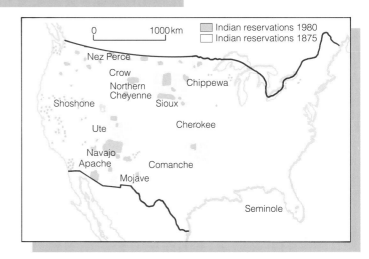

called 'avenues', like Madison Avenue and Fifth Avenue, go north to south and the streets go east to west.

New York, like most American cities, has many problems. Although people work in the city centre, those with money prefer to live in the suburbs and commute daily. This causes traffic congestion and air pollution. Around the centre, where the offices are located, are the older houses and flats which were the early suburbs. These have become GHETTOES for the poor and underprivileged. The housing conditions are appalling with some people living in

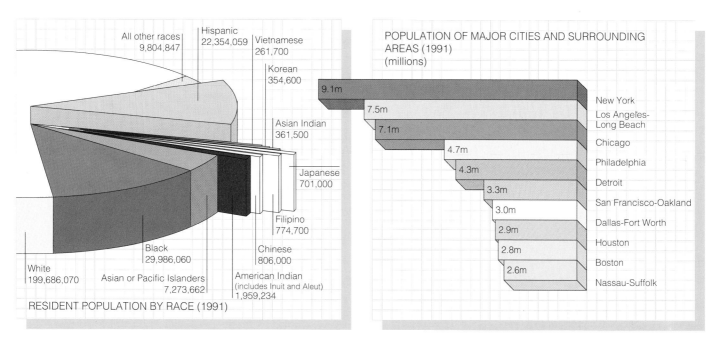

RESIDENT POPULATION BY RACE (1991)

- All other races 9,804,847
- Hispanic 22,354,059
- Vietnamese 261,700
- Korean 354,600
- Asian Indian 361,500
- Japanese 701,000
- Filipino 774,700
- Chinese 806,000
- American Indian (includes Inuit and Aleut) 1,959,234
- Black 29,986,060
- Asian or Pacific Islanders 7,273,662
- White 199,686,070

POPULATION OF MAJOR CITIES AND SURROUNDING AREAS (1991) (millions)

- New York 9.1m
- Los Angeles-Long Beach 7.5m
- Chicago 7.1m
- Philadelphia 4.7m
- Detroit 4.3m
- San Francisco-Oakland 3.3m
- Dallas-Fort Worth 3.0m
- Houston 2.9m
- Boston 2.8m
- Nassau-Suffolk 2.6m

buildings condemned 90 years ago. There is a lot of unemployment and crime. Firms are moving away to more pleasant surroundings adding to the city's unemployment problems.

People are trying to solve the problems. For example, Boston has redeveloped its centre so that it provides a pleasant and safe environment for people. As a result it is attracting new businesses and the city centre has become prosperous again.

RURAL LIVING

Outside these major conurbations, the density of population is very low and there is a lot of open space. In sharp contrast to the wealth of the cities, many rural communities are very poor — for both white and black Americans.

▶ *Telluride in Colorado is typical of the many small towns that are found across the USA. There is little more than a main street with a few shops and offices.*

FAMILY LIFE

American families are generally small and, compared with most other countries, very well off. The American dream so often portrayed by advertisers and in TV programmes is a middle-class family consisting of mother, father and two children living in a detached suburban house filled with modern consumer goods. However, one-quarter of all American children live with only one parent. This is because the divorce rate is high with almost one in two marriages ending in divorce.

The average income per head is $19,815, about fifty times that of a country like Pakistan. Half of all young mothers go out to work. Virtually all homes have electricity, fridges and televisions. There are two radios for every person, one TV to 1.2 people and one telephone to 1.3 people. With 1 car to every 1.8 people, the USA has the highest car ownership in the world. The average working week is 41 hours, higher than in most developed countries but less than in poorer countries.

EDUCATION

Families consider education to be very important. Each state is responsible for providing schooling. In general school is compulsory between the ages of 7 and 16. However, 95 per cent of all 5 and 6-year-olds go to school and 34 per cent of 18 to 24-year-olds are at colleges and universities improving their qualifications. Equal numbers of young men and women stay on beyond the compulsory school age. Women have better qualifications than men but only 3 per cent of top managers are women.

Children study a wide variety of subjects. Schools also encourage children to learn

RELIGIOUS DAYS AND HOLIDAYS	
January 1	New Year's Day
January 15	Martin Luther King's Day celebrates the life of the black civil rights leader
February 19 or 22	Washington's Birthday, the first President of the United States of America
May 28	Memorial Day
July 4	Independence Day
September 3	Labor Day
October 8 or 12	Columbus Day
November 11	Veterans' Day
November 22	Thanksgiving
December 25	Christmas Day

◀ *Luxurious mobile homes (camper vans) are used by families for touring the USA's many wild areas.*

20

KEY FACTS

● 60% of American homes are detached.
● 33,800 people in New York are homeless.
● 12% of Americans are over 65. In Miami, 17% of the population is over 65 because many move there when they retire.
● The Astrodome sports stadium in Houston, Texas, which seats 50,000 people is completely enclosed and large enough for a baseball match.
● Jane Fonda's workout book has sold over 1 million copies.
● There are over 9,600 radio stations, 1,092 television stations and 1,611 daily newspapers.
● The average American viewer is likely to see 15 murders a week on entertainment programmes.

▲ *Every big city wants to have a famous football team. Local people follow their teams fervently and the razzamataz before a match is almost as important as the game itself.*

about their own cultural backgrounds, although few schools teach foreign languages or religion. Some children are bussed out of their home area so that schools can have mixed ethnic groups. Education is free except at private schools. About 11 per cent of children go to private schools which are most common in New England.

There are two very famous universities. Harvard was founded in 1636 at Cambridge in Massachusetts. Yale was founded in 1701 at New Haven in Connecticut.

◀Harlem is an area of New York where many poor Black Americans live. Employment is hard to find. Violent crime and drug abuse are common. New York has 23 murders a year for every 100,000 people.

SOCIAL PROBLEMS

The USA has many social problems that are linked to poverty. White Americans are the wealthiest group and only about 10 per cent live below the poverty line. More than 30 per cent of Non-whites live below it. The standard of living of American Indians is only half that of White Americans. They have lost their lands, their livelihoods and their culture and, for some, alcohol is the only substitute.

In the big cities like New York and Chicago, the poor live in ghettoes where conditions are atrocious. The life expectancy of people living in the ghettoes may be only 53 – as low as in a developing country like Bangladesh. The average number of murders in the USA is 8.7 a year for every 100,000 people. That is four times higher than in western Europe.

LEISURE

The Americans have invented three major sports: basketball, baseball and American

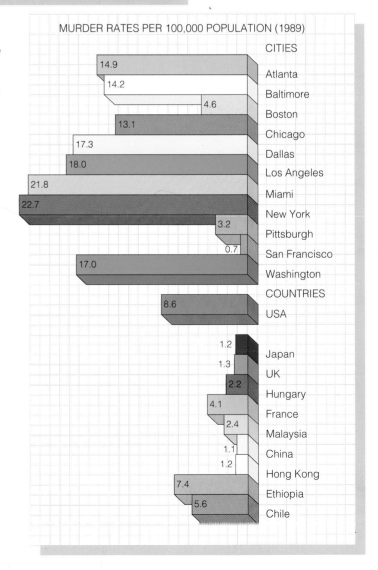

MURDER RATES PER 100,000 POPULATION (1989)

CITIES

Atlanta	14.9
Baltimore	14.2
Boston	4.6
Chicago	13.1
Dallas	17.3
Los Angeles	18.0
Miami	21.8
New York	22.7
Pittsburgh	3.2
San Francisco	0.7
Washington	17.0

COUNTRIES

Country	Rate
USA	8.6
Japan	1.2
UK	1.3
Hungary	2.2
France	4.1
Malaysia	2.4
China	1.1
Hong Kong	1.2
Ethiopia	7.4
Chile	5.6

► *Bright yellow buses like those in the picture can be seen all over the USA. They are school buses and are used to take children to and from school and on study trips.*

football. Baseball is the most popular and about 53 million people a year go to matches. Millions more watch them on television. Another occasion unique to North America is the rodeo where cowboys show their skills.

The favourite leisure activity is watching television. There are 1,000 TV stations, although most are local rather than national. Viewers have more choice than anywhere else in the world.

People enjoy eating out. America introduced the world to 'fast food' through such food chains as McDonald's and Kentucky Fried Chicken. However, more Americans are becoming more health conscious and are jogging, joining health clubs and eating more healthily.

RELIGION

America is a Christian country with 87 per cent of people saying they are Christian and 40 per cent going to church regularly. Churches run 200 TV stations and 3 networks and their programmes are seen by 60 million people a week. They raise a lot of money to build hospitals, universities and even theme parks. Other religions represented are Jewish (2.7%), Muslim (1.9%) and Hindu (0.2%).

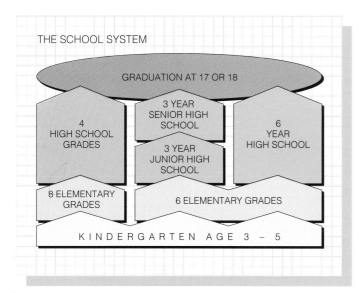

THE SCHOOL SYSTEM

GRADUATION AT 17 OR 18

4 HIGH SCHOOL GRADES

3 YEAR SENIOR HIGH SCHOOL

6 YEAR HIGH SCHOOL

3 YEAR JUNIOR HIGH SCHOOL

8 ELEMENTARY GRADES

6 ELEMENTARY GRADES

KINDERGARTEN AGE 3 – 5

◄ *Education is the responsibility of each state and there are three main systems. However, the curriculum is very similar throughout the country.*

In 1776 thirteen British colonies in North America declared they were the independent nation called the United States of America. In 1781, led by George Washington, they won the War of Independence against Britain. In 1789 the Constitution that remains to this day was agreed.

Other states joined the original thirteen, but between 1861 and 1865 the country almost broke up. The Civil War occurred because the states in the South wanted to continue with slavery but the North wanted to abolish it. The North won and slavery was abolished.

Each state has its own government which makes its own laws relating to taxes, law courts, the police force and education. The laws must not contradict the Constitution of the USA. The people elect a governor and

▲ **The White House in Washington DC is the President's home and office. Washington DC became the capital and seat of government in 1800.**

KEY FACTS

● George Washington was the first President of the USA.
● The DC in Washington DC stands for District of Columbia.
● 600,000 people were killed in the Civil War.
● The USA bought Alaska from the Russians in 1867.
● The USA is home to the United Nations and many of its agencies, including the World Bank.

▶ *The two main political parties spend millions of dollars on campaigning. They use all the modern media techniques, including television advertising. The big presidential rallies are like a Hollywood extravaganza.*

GOVERNMENT OF THE USA

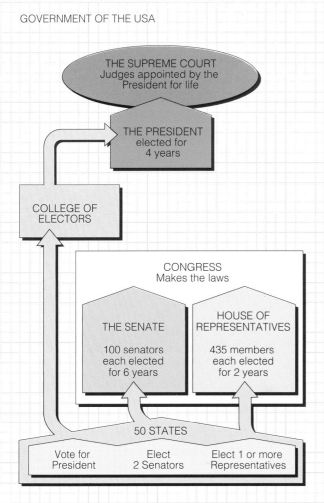

◀ *The government of the USA is headed by the President. He is responsible for carrying out the laws of the land.*

people to make the laws.

National laws are made by Congress. Congress is made up of the Senate and the House of Representatives. Each state elects two Senators to the Senate and one or more Representatives, depending on the population of the state, to the House of Representatives.

The Supreme Court makes sure that no laws contradict the Constitution.

The President is elected by the College of Electors. Each state instructs its electors which presidential candidate to vote for.

There are two main parties, the Republicans and the Democrats. They put forward people for election to all areas of public life, from town councils to the presidency. In the first stage of an election, the people vote for the candidate they want their party to put forward. In the second stage they vote for whichever candidate they prefer.

FOOD AND FARMING

Arable

Fruit and vegetables

Grazing

Forest with arable and pasture

Non-agricultural land

► *Farming varies considerably across the USA because of the many different climate and soil conditions.*

Farming in the USA is very efficient. Not only can farmers produce enough food for everyone, they also export it to other countries. Farm products account for 8 per cent of American exports. The USA produces 14 per cent of the world's wheat and 46 per cent of its maize (known as corn in the USA). However, this huge production only employs 3 per cent of the labour force because farmers use the latest agricultural machinery and chemicals.

In Florida the sub-tropical climate is ideal for growing citrus fruits such as oranges. It produces one-third of all citrus fruits in the USA. Oranges are the most important crop and most are made into orange juice. Oranges for eating usually come from California.

Another plantation crop is cotton. It is grown in all the southern states from California to South Carolina but it is no longer as dominant as it used to be as other crops, such as soya beans, are now grown.

The main food producing area lies in the north between the Rocky Mountains and the

▼ *The huge flat fields of Minnesota are ideal for big machines. These combine harvesters can cut enough wheat in an hour to feed a family for 40 years.*

FOOD INTAKE IN CALORIES PER DAY	
USA	3642
Belgium	3850
Germany	3800
UK	3257
Japan	2858
China	2628
India	2204
Bangladesh	1922

▲ *These water sprinklers mean the desert can grow grops. They move round in circles and from the air irrigated areas stand out as huge green circles.*

Appalachians. South of the Great Lakes maize is the main crop, usually grown in rotation with soya beans. About 90 per cent of the maize is fed to animals and the area produces half of all the pigs in the USA.

To the west more wheat is grown. The climate is really too dry and the summers too short for growing wheat, but by developing wheat that will grow fast and not die if there is too little rain, production has increased. The USA exports about 30 million tonnes of wheat a year.

The main ranching areas are further west, stretching from North Dakota to Texas where it is too dry for growing crops. It was from this area that the legends of the Wild West developed. Today 'producers' rear calves on the Plains and sell them to 'feeders' who fatten them up in huge pens ready for slaughter. Meat is an important part of an American's diet, whether it is a thick steak or a hamburger.

Central Valley in California has become the main area producing fruit, flowers and vegetables although the area hardly receives any rainfall. All the major rivers

Californian wines are famous throughout the world. Napa Valley is one of the main grape-growing areas.

Tending the vines is still best done by humans, though machines pick the grapes.

flowing into the Sacramento and San Joaquin rivers are dammed and the water led through a network of canals to irrigate an area that is semi-desert. Products are sent to most parts of the USA.

In Alaska, where the climate is too harsh for growing crops, fishing is very important, but the numbers of fish have declined because too many have been caught.

KEY FACTS

● Americans eat about 50 kilos of meat a year compared with 23 kilos eaten by Europeans.
● California produces almost half the USA's fruit and vegetables.
● The USA produces 7 million tonnes of oranges a year.
● The USA has 1,550 million poultry, 99 million cattle and 55.5 million pigs.
● One Alaskan speciality is the king crab which measures 2 metres from claw to claw.

TRADE AND INDUSTRY

◀San Francisco has one of the most picturesque harbours in the world. The Golden Gate Bridge spans the entrance to the San Francisco Bay.

The industries of the USA and Japan each produce twice as much as Germany, the third highest producer.

MANUFACTURING INDUSTRY

Industry has always been important to the Americans. Importing goods from Europe was expensive and the country had a wealth of minerals and energy supplies that it could use to make products for itself. The American flair for enterprise has helped the growth of industry. Alexander Graham Bell invented the telephone and now all countries have telephone systems. Henry

IMPORTS FROM (1989) (%)

Others — Italy 2.5 — France 2.8
China
27.4
UK 3.9
S Korea 4.2
2.5
2.1
19.8
Taiwan 5.1
5.3
18.6
5.8
Hong Kong
Japan
Germany
Mexico
Canada

EXPORTS TO (%)

Australia 2.3
Belgium/Luxembourg 2.3
Others — Taiwan 3.1 — Netherlands 3.1
France 3.2
29.3
S Korea 3.7
4.6
2.0
21.6
12.2
6.9
5.7
Canada
Japan
UK
Mexico
Singapore
Germany

SHARE OF WORLD TRADE 1989 (%)

USA Japan Germany
10.43 11.09
14.88

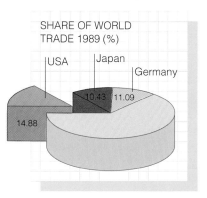

◀The USA is the world's biggest trading nation.

▶The USA trades with most countries.

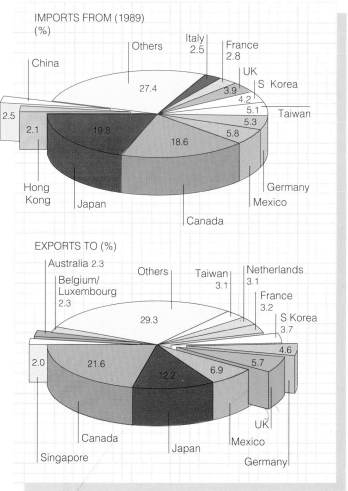

KEY FACTS

- Boeing, based in Seattle, produces half of all the world's airliners.
- Paramount pictures is now owned by a Japanese company.
- *Robin, Prince of Thieves* cost $55 million to make and in the USA alone made $165 million in the first year.
- In 1989 American factories produced 24.8 million television sets, 10.8 million vehicles, 10.5 million microwave ovens, 7 million refrigerators and 6.2 million washing machines.

▲ **The USA is the main supplier of aircraft to the world's airlines. This factory at Everett, Washington, produces Boeing aircraft – the world's most popular passenger planes.**

Ford introduced the first assembly line to build his cars more cheaply, and now most goods are produced in this way. American industries are world leaders in many areas including aerospace, micro-electronics and medicines. Manufacturing employs about 19 million people, more than a quarter of all working people.

One of the most important products a wealthy industrial country needs is steel. It is used by the building, engineering and manufacturing industries. The USA produces about 98 million tonnes a year compared with 106 million tonnes in Japan and 19 million tonnes in Britain. Almost 10 per cent of the production comes from the plant at Sparrow's Point on Chesapeake Bay. Most other plants are in the region between Pittsburgh and Chicago where good transport facilities bring together the two raw materials, coal and iron ore, easily.

This area of the Mid-west is also the main manufacturing region. It produces consumer goods like cookers and freezers, but the most important single industry is the manufacture of vehicles and vehicle parts. Detroit is the 'Motor Town' or 'Motown' of the USA, although many cars are now assembled in other parts of the country from parts made in the Detroit area.

The principal industries have changed over the years. At the beginning of the century the main industries were textiles, clothing, tobacco, leather, products made from oil, making metals like iron and steel and transport equipment. Many of these traditional industries have found it difficult to compete with goods made in the Far East, especially in Japan, Taiwan and South Korea. For example, the number of imported cars has risen from just over 2 million in 1970 to almost 4.5 million a year today – more than half of all new cars. Many factories have closed, giving the region the name of 'the rust belt'. Unemployment is high.

High-tech industries such as micro-electronics are the fastest growing industries today. They are often called 'sunrise' industries because they are bringing about the dawn of the new Information Age. The area between San Francisco Bay and the Santa Cruz Mountains has become known as Silicon Valley because all along Highway 280 there are factories developing and manufacturing components for all types of computers and computer-controlled equipment. The silicon chip is the basis of these industries.

The area around the Gulf of Mexico is also an important industrial area, especially for oil refining and chemicals. Since the space programme set up its headquarters at Houston, Texas, many new computer and aerospace industries have developed. For example, rockets are made in New Orleans and taken to Cape Canaveral in Florida for launching.

USING ENERGY

The American way of life is dependent on using large amounts of energy, especially energy from oil. The average American consumes almost twice as much energy as the average European. Supplies will only last another 50 years at most, so industry needs to find alternative sources of energy. Hydro-electric power provides about 9 per cent and nuclear power 17 per cent of electrical power. Even wind and solar power are being used but they contribute only small amounts of energy. For example, the wind farms in California only provide 1 per cent of the electrical energy needed by the state.

EMPLOYMENT IN USA 1989 (%)

Agriculture | Industry
27.1
3
67.7
Services

▶ *This oil refinery in Texas is typical of many around the Gulf of Mexico.*

AMERICAN COMPANIES

Many companies that originated in the USA have become household names all around the world: Coca Cola, Pepsi, McDonald's, Pizza Hut, IBM, Kodak, Ford, General Motors, Paramount, Hoover, Esso, Texaco and so on. The largest American company is General Motors which sold goods worth $126 billion in 1990.

As well as large businesses there are many small ones in the USA. They are very important to the economy and employ about half of all American workers. Many of these businesses are franchises. A large company, such as McDonald's or Burger King, allows a person to set up a business using their name and selling their goods. The company provides the products like hamburgers and fries, does the advertising and makes sure the individual outlets all do their business the company way. The owner of the business pays a fee to get started and a small part of the profits afterwards. McDonald's is the largest franchise in the USA, with 7,919 outlets in 1990.

SERVICE INDUSTRIES

Manufacturing industries create the most wealth and are expanding but they employ far fewer people than 40 years ago because many of the jobs have been automated. Today 68 per cent of working people are employed in service industries such as shops, restaurants, garages, insurance offices, film and television, and tourism.

The Hollywood area of Los Angeles is the centre of the film and television industry. The warm, sunny climate was ideal for making films outdoors and although that is not so important today because many are made on sets, Hollywood has remained the centre of the industry. American films and programmes are shown all over the world, often with sub-titles or dubbed into other languages. *Terminator 2*, one of the most popular films of 1991, made $201 million in the USA and £19 million in Britain within a few months of being released.

◀*The USA is the leading country designing and making miniaturised electrical circuits that are used in computers and computer-controlled machines. Many of these high-tech industries are located south of San Francisco in Silicon Valley.*

▶*The American space programme put the first man on the moon and built the first space shuttle. The vehicle goes into orbit like a rocket and then returns to the Earth like an aircraft. The photo shows Discovery being launched from Cape Canaveral in Florida.*

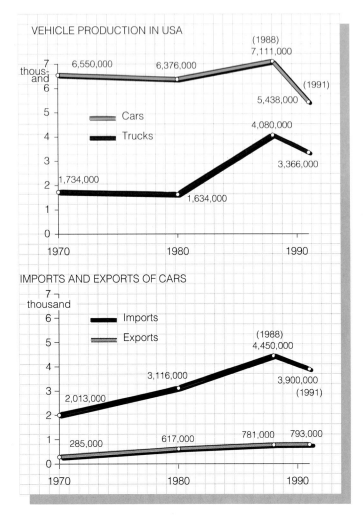

VEHICLE PRODUCTION IN USA

Cars
Trucks

6,550,000 6,376,000 (1988) 7,111,000 (1991) 5,438,000

1,734,000 1,634,000 4,080,000 3,366,000

IMPORTS AND EXPORTS OF CARS

Imports
Exports

2,013,000 3,116,000 (1988) 4,450,000 3,900,000 (1991)

285,000 617,000 781,000 793,000

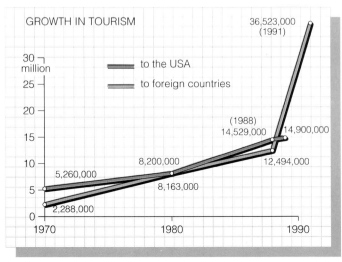

GROWTH IN TOURISM

to the USA
to foreign countries

36,523,000 (1991)

(1988) 14,529,000 14,900,000

5,260,000 8,200,000 12,494,000

2,288,000 8,163,000

The tourist industry becomes more important as people become richer and have more time to travel. One of the most popular places to visit is Florida, also known as the Sunshine State. It is very popular with northern visitors in winter. Florida has the popular beaches of Miami and more than 20 or so major attractions around Orlando including Disneyworld and Universal Studios, two of the most famous theme parks in the world. Disneyworld has over 14 million visitors a year from the USA and other countries.

The USA is becoming a popular destination for tourists from overseas because the cost of air travel has fallen. Of the 12.5 million overseas visitors, 5.5 million come from western Europe and Florida is one of the most popular destinations. Visitors spend about $34 billion a year in the USA but this is just about equalled by the amount that American tourists spend abroad. Europe is the most popular destination, receiving about 7 million American tourists a year.

AMERICAN TRADE

The USA has become a major trading country and its government believes that all countries should be able to sell things to each other without any restrictions. The USA earns more money from the goods it exports than any other country, averaging around $320 billion a year. However, it spends far more on buying imports than it earns from exports and has the largest TRADE DEFICIT in the world at around $140 billion. Japan has the largest TRADE SURPLUS with the USA and is investing a lot of this money in American businesses. Japanese companies now own many American businesses as well as real estate.

The major exports are goods that Americans make. Products made by other countries are the major imports. Most

▶ *Shares in American companies are traded at the Stock Exchange, Wall Street, New York. With London and Tokyo, it is one of the big three stock exchanges.*

trade is done with Canada, Japan and Mexico. Cars, mainly from Japan and Europe, account for 15 per cent of all the manufactured goods that are imported. Others include televisions, radios, sound and video systems and electronic goods. The manufactured goods exported include computer and office equipment, aircraft and motor vehicles.

THE WORKFORCE

The number of women who go out to work has doubled over the past 30 years. Women now make up half the workforce. However, they generally earn less than men even when they are doing similar jobs. There are very few women at the top of the big companies, but women are doing jobs that traditionally have only been done by men. For example, in 1975 all airline pilots were men. Today, one in 20 is a woman. There are also more women working as economists, lawyers, judges and computer programmers.

The USA is so big that transport is extremely important. It employs about 10 per cent of the workforce.

Boats and barges moving around the coast, along the Mississippi river system and across the Great Lakes were the earliest ways of moving large quantities of goods. Water transport is still important today. It accounts for 37 per cent of all freight carried. New Orleans at the end of the Mississippi is the largest port, handling over 175 million tonnes a year.

The railways were built across the country to help the development of the West. They carried goods and people, but today they are mainly used to carry bulky goods such as coal and wheat. They account for 27 per cent of freight carried. The rail network is 278,245 kilometres long, the second largest in the world after the former Soviet Union. The main railway company is Amtrak.

▲ *The USA is a large country and goods have to be carried great distances. Trains can be over a kilometre long.*

There are about 42 million road trucks in the USA and they carry 19 per cent of the freight. Some are very large and carry goods very long distances. There is an excellent road system with 3.8 million kilometres of roads.

The USA needs a good road network because Americans are great travellers and go almost everywhere by car. The towns and the suburbs are designed around the car and

KEY FACTS

● 80 per cent of downtown Los Angeles is devoted to the car, such as roads, parking places, garages.
● In Los Angeles there are 90 cars for every 100 people old enough to drive.

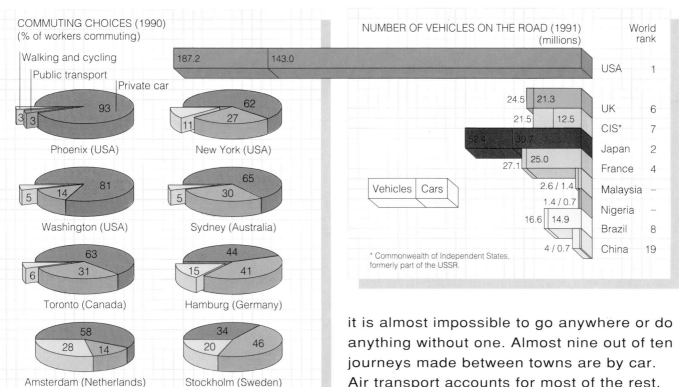

COMMUTING CHOICES (1990)
(% of workers commuting)

Walking and cycling
Public transport
Private car

Phoenix (USA): 93 / 3 / 3	New York (USA): 62 / 27 / 11
Washington (USA): 81 / 14 / 5	Sydney (Australia): 65 / 30 / 5
Toronto (Canada): 63 / 31 / 6	Hamburg (Germany): 44 / 41 / 15
Amsterdam (Netherlands): 58 / 14 / 28	Stockholm (Sweden): 34 / 46 / 20
Munich (Germany): 38 / 42 / 20	Vienna (Austria): 40 / 45 / 15
Tokyo (Japan): 16 / 59 / 25	Hong Kong: 62 / 35 / 3

NUMBER OF VEHICLES ON THE ROAD (1991)
(millions)

Vehicles | Cars

Country	Vehicles	Cars	World rank
USA	187.2	143.0	1
UK	24.5	21.3	6
CIS*	21.5	12.5	7
Japan	52.4	30.7	2
France	27.1	25.0	4
Malaysia	2.6	1.4	–
Nigeria	1.4	0.7	–
Brazil	16.6	14.9	8
China	4	0.7	19

* Commonwealth of Independent States,
formerly part of the USSR.

it is almost impossible to go anywhere or do anything without one. Almost nine out of ten journeys made between towns are by car. Air transport accounts for most of the rest. Because of the size of the country, air travel is very important. It is fast, quite cheap and as easy to use as a bus. It is very popular for business travel.

Americans depend on their cars, but with almost 7 million new cars a year being bought they cause many problems, especially traffic congestion and air pollution in the main cities.

▶ *The Bay Area Rapid Transit system (BART) was built to ease congestion on San Francisco's roads. The 11 kilometre journey from Oakland takes 9 minutes instead of 40 minutes by road in the rush hours.*

THE ENVIRONMENT

The American way of life has many benefits, but it causes serious environmental problems. It was not until Earth Day 1969 that Americans started to consider seriously doing something to solve these problems. Sewage and chemicals from factories were killing wildlife in rivers. Large cities were regularly enveloped in smog. Cities were taking up more and more land. Mines were damaging the landscape and farmers were turning more and more wild areas into farmland.

GARBAGE

Americans are the world's major consumers. They are also the major producers of rubbish (knows as garbage in the USA). Every day, each person produces about 1.8 kilos of rubbish such as paper, bottles and glass. The amount doubled between 1960 and 1988 to almost 180 million tonnes a year. Although it contains valuable raw materials, most of the rubbish is buried or burnt. Only 14 per cent is recycled.

AIR POLLUTION

Air pollution is a serious problem especially in and near big cities. Polluted air is unhealthy to breathe and damages

▲ *Dawn over Los Angeles and the haze caused by pollution is clearly visible. In 1989 the air was considered unhealthy to breathe on 206 days.*

buildings and wildlife. Pollution can be carried hundreds of kilometres in the wind and fall as acid rain. Acid rain has killed wildlife in a quarter of the lakes in the Adirondack Mountains of New York State.

WATER POLLUTION

Rivers and the sea around the coast are badly polluted with sewage and industrial chemicals. In 1969 the Cuyahoga river in Ohio was so full of oil, chemicals and debris

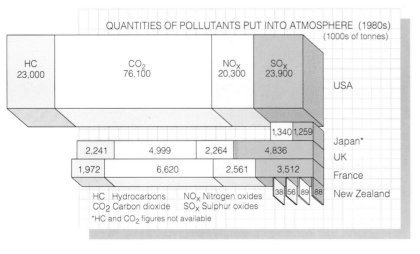

QUANTITIES OF POLLUTANTS PUT INTO ATMOSPHERE (1980s)
(1000s of tonnes)

	HC	CO₂	NOₓ	SOₓ	
USA	23,000	76,100	20,300	23,900	
Japan*			1,340	1,259	
UK	2,241	4,999	2,264	4,836	
France	1,972	6,620	2,561	3,512	
New Zealand	38	56	89	88	

HC Hydrocarbons   NOₓ Nitrogen oxides
CO₂ Carbon dioxide   SOₓ Sulphur oxides
*HC and CO₂ figures not available

KEY FACTS

● 90% of petrol sold in the USA is unleaded.

● Only 1% of the plastics used in the USA are recycled.

● The USA produces 19% of all the world's waste.

● Americans use 80 billion aluminium cans a year – 16 cans for every person in the world.

● More than three million people a year visit Yosemite National Park.

● 90% of ancient forest in the north-west has been chopped down.

that it caught fire. Laws were passed in the 1970s to prevent water pollution but they are not always being obeyed. Over 30 cities on the east coast still pump untreated sewage into the sea. Pollution damages fish and other animals in the sea. One-third of the oyster beds off Louisiana and half of the shellfish beds of Texas have had to be closed because the food from them is too poisonous to eat.

WILDLIFE AT RISK

Large areas of the USA have been changed by farmers, foresters and builders. Every year 1 million hectares of land are taken over for roads, towns and industry. As a result there are fewer natural areas for wild plants and animals to live. For example, the

▲ *The Yosemite National Park covers 3,061 square kilometres in central California. It has spectacular scenery and many lakes, rivers and waterfalls.*

prairies were once home to 60 million bison, but hunting, ranching and cereal farming reduced them to 300 by 1890. Waterlogged areas are particularly valuable for wildlife but excluding Alaska, 75 per cent of these areas have been destroyed by farming or other uses.

Many species of wildlife are in danger of becoming extinct, including America's national bird, the bald eagle. In 1991, 216 species of American animals and 180 species of American plants were listed as being in danger.

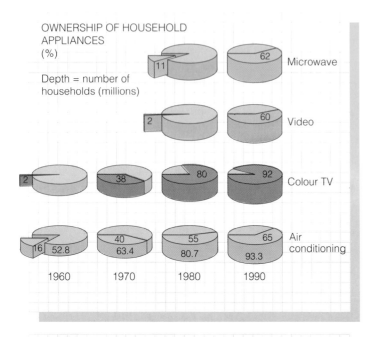

OWNERSHIP OF HOUSEHOLD
APPLIANCES
(%)

Depth = number of
households (millions)

Microwave — 11, 62

Video — 2, 60

Colour TV — 2, 38, 80, 92

Air conditioning — 16 52.8, 40 63.4, 55 80.7, 65 93.3

1960 1970 1980 1990

SOIL DAMAGE

Farmers depend on the soil but since farming began in the USA one-third of the top soil has been lost. Keeping too many cattle on rangelands, removing forests from slopes, growing the same crop year after year and dry weather conditions have created conditions in which the wind and rain can carry away the soil. Where irrigation is used, the hot weather brings salts to the surface of the soil. Plants cannot grow where the salts are found, so the soil becomes useless.

PROTECTION FOR THE ENVIRONMENT

Today, Americans are very well informed about environmental problems and many belong to environmental organizations which are trying to protect the environment. The National Wildlife Federation has 5.8 million members, Greenpeace USA 2.3 million members and the Sierra Club 633,000.

One way of protecting beautiful scenery and wildlife is to set up national parks where people are not allowed to live and there are no factories, major roads or airports. Hunting is forbidden. Yellowstone

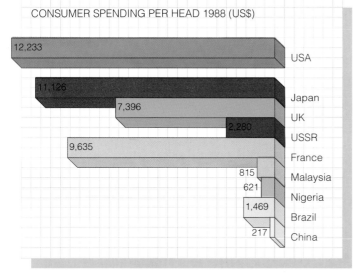

CONSUMER SPENDING PER HEAD 1988 (US$)

Country	US$
USA	12,233
Japan	11,126
UK	7,396
USSR	2,280
France	9,635
Malaysia	815
Nigeria	621
Brazil	1,469
China	217

178,000,000 — USA
41,530,000 — Japan
16,668,000 — UK
15,000,000 — France

SOLID HOUSEHOLD WASTE PRODUCED (1980s)
(tonnes)

NUMBER OF PEOPLE PER (1988)	CAR	TV	PHONE	RADIO
USA	1.8	1.2	1.3	0.5
Japan	4.2	1.7	1.8	1.2
UK	2.8	2.8	1.9	3.0
USSR	22.8	9.4	10.3	4.4
France	2.5	2.7	1.6	2.7
Malaysia	14.1	9.0	11.7	2.3
Nigeria	144.8	179.1	366.7	6.1
Brazil	15.8	5.2	11.3	2.7
China	1,093.0	100.7	149.8	7.1

in the Rockies was the world's first national park. It was set up in 1872. It is half the size of Wales and the largest in the USA. There are 38 parks now but many, such as Yosemite in California, have become so popular that they are getting overcrowded. Today cars are only allowed to reach a few places. Camp sites have to be booked in advance and the number of walkers allowed on the trails is controlled.

The government has set up the Environmental Protection Agency and it is helping to make and enforce the environmental laws. Individual states also make their own laws.

Pollution is being controlled and the quality of the air is slowly improving. For example, the quantity of carbon monoxide going into the air fell from 79.6 million tonnes in 1980 to 60.9 million tonnes in 1989. New cars create much less pollution than older models. Where there are open-cast mines the land has to be restored when the minerals are worked out. In California building on agricultural land is being prevented to stop the cities from spreading. Schemes to recycle paper, glass and metals are becoming more popular. In 1960 only 18 per cent of old paper and 1.5 per cent of glass were recycled. By 1988 these figures had risen to 26 per cent for paper and 12 per cent for glass.

▼ *Many people feel strongly that more should be done to protect the environment. This is an 'Earth Day' demonstration in New York.*

THE FURTURE

The USA may be the richest and most powerful country in the world but it still has to plan for its future.

There are major social problems caused by poverty and many people have lost faith in the 'American Dream' and turned to drugs and crime. The way of life causes much damage to the environment and more attention must be paid to

▶ *Is the bald eagle a symbol of the future for the USA? Hunting and pesticide poisoning almost made it extinct, but conservationists are now protecting it.*

◀ *This painting on the wall in a poor inner city area looks forward to a time when all people can live together in peace and harmony.*

conservation. New jobs need to be created as automation replaces jobs and American industry finds it difficult to compete with industries abroad.

Many countries are opposed to the USA because it has so much influence. However, they also expect it to use its wealth and influence to help solve many of the world's problems. It is not easy being the most powerful country in the world.

KEY FACTS

● The number of people living to over 100 is expected to rise from 56,000 in 1990 to 266,000 in 2020. A fivefold increase.
● Spending on the environment is likely to increase from $19 billion a year in 1987 to $32 billion a year in 2000.

FURTHER INFORMATION

THE STATES OF THE USA

STATE	DATE JOINED USA	CAPITAL	AREA (SQ KM)	POPULATION
Alabama	1819	Montgomery	133,915	4,062,608
Alaska	1959	Juneau	1,530,693	551,947
Arizona	1912	Phoenix	295,259	3,677,985
Arkansas	1836	Little Rock	137,754	2,362,239
California	1850	Sacramento	411,047	29,839,250
Colorado	1876	Denver	269,594	3,307,912
Connecticut	1788	Hartford	12,997	3,295,669
Delaware	1787	Dover	5,294	668,696
Florida	1845	Tallahassee	151,939	13,003,362
Georgia	1788	Atlanta	152,576	6,508,419
Hawaii	1959	Honolulu	16,760	1,115,274
Idaho	1890	Boise	216,430	1,011,986
Illinois	1818	Springfield	149,885	11,466,682
Indiana	1816	Indianapolis	94,309	5,564,228
Iowa	1846	Des Moines	145,752	2,787,424
Kansas	1861	Topeka	213,096	2,485,600
Kentucky	1792	Frankfort	104,659	3,698,969
Louisiana	1812	Baton Rouge	123,677	4,238,216
Maine	1820	Augusta	86,156	1,233,223
Maryland	1788	Annapolis	27,091	4,798,622
Massachusetts	1788	Boston	21,455	6,029,051
Michigan	1837	Lansing	251,493	9,328,784
Minnesota	1858	St Paul	224,329	4,387,029
Mississippi	1817	Jackson	123,514	2,586,443
Missouri	1821	Jefferson City	180,514	5,137,804
Montana	1889	Helena	380,847	803,655
Nebraska	1867	Lincoln	200,349	1,584,617
Nevada	1864	Carson City	286,352	1,206,152
New Hampshire	1788	Concord	24,032	1,113,915
New Jersey	1787	Trenton	20,168	7,748,634
New Mexico	1912	Santa Fé	314,924	1,521,779
New York	1788	Albany	136,593	18,044,505
North Carolina	1789	Raleigh	136,412	6,657,630
North Dakota	1889	Bismarck	183,117	641,364
Ohio	1803	Columbus	115,998	10,887,325
Oklahoma	1907	Oklahoma City	181,185	3,157,604
Oregon	1859	Salem	251,418	2,853,733
Pennsylvania	1787	Harrisburg	119,251	11,924,710
Rhode Island	1790	Providence	3,139	1,005,984
South Carolina	1788	Columbia	80,582	3,505,707
South Dakota	1889	Pierre	199,730	699,999
Tennessee	1796	Nashville	109,152	4,896,641
Texas	1845	Austin	691,027	17,059,805
Utah	1896	Salt Lake City	219,887	1,727,784
Vermont	1791	Montpelier	24,900	564,964
Virginia	1788	Richmond	105,566	6,216,568
Washington	1889	Olympia	176,479	4,887,941
West Virginia	1863	Charleston	62,758	1,801,625
Wisconsin	1848	Madison	171,496	4,906,745
Wyoming	1890	Cheyenne	253,324	455,975
District of Columbia	1791	—	179	609,909

US INFORMATION SERVICE,
US Embassy, 24 Grosvenor Square,
London W1
The US Embassy's Information Service is
an excellent source of information, facts
and statistics about all aspects of life in the
USA.
US TRAVEL AND TOURISM
ADMINISTRATION,
22 Sackville Street, London W1X 2EA
For information of a more general nature
about places and the countryside, from
Disneyworld to the Yosemite National Park.

BOOKS ABOUT THE USA
United States, Passport Series, Keith Lye,
Franklin Watts 1989 (age 8–12)
The USA, Countries of the World Series,
Pam Cary, Wayland 1988 (age 8–12)
The USA since 1945, Witness History
Series, Nigel Smith, Wayland 1988
(age 12–14)

GLOSSARY

CAPITALISM
A way of life in which individuals own
businesses and run them to try to make a
profit.

CONURBATION
A large built-up area formed when several
towns spread out over the countryside and
join up.

DEMOCRACY
A country which is governed by the
politicians elected by the people of that
country.

GHETTO
A densely populated slum area in a city
where poor people live and living conditions
are very bad.

OPEN-CAST MINING
Mining in which huge holes are dug to reach
valuable minerals below the surface.

TRADE DEFICIT
When the value of goods imported by a
country is worth more than the value of
goods exported. This is similar to people
spending more money than they earn.

TRADE SURPLUS
When the value of goods exported by a
country is worth more than the value of
goods imported.

INDEX

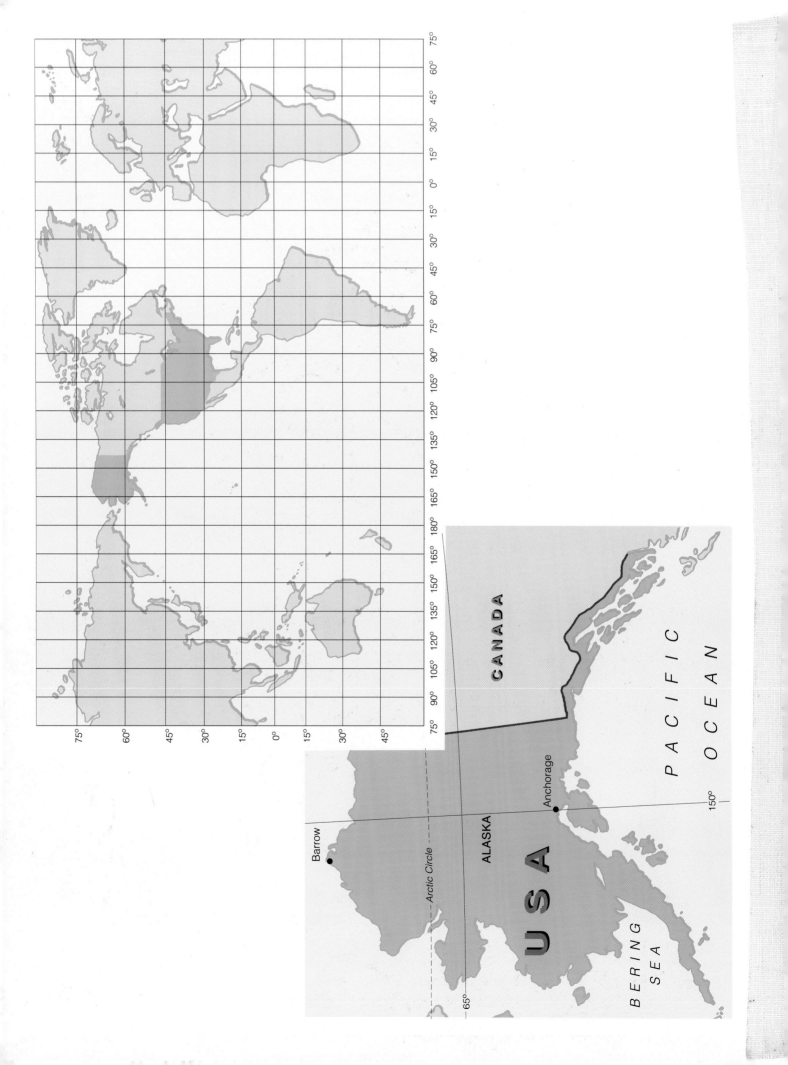

75°
60°
45°
30°
15°
0°
15°
30°
45°

75°   60°   45°   30°   15°   0°   15°   30°   75°

75°
60°
45°
30°
15°
0°
15°
30°
45°
60°
75°

105°   120°   135°   150°   165°   180°   165°   150°   135°   120°   105°   90°   75°

CANADA

ALASKA

USA

Barrow

Arctic Circle

Anchorage

65°

150°

BERING
SEA

PACIFIC

OCEAN